Birdhouses & Feeders

GREG CHEETHAM

CONTENTS

Sharing your garden with birds   4

Hanging birdhouse   10

Open-sided feeder   16

Gabled birdhouse   22

Birdhouse with hinged lid   28

Dovecote   34

Hollow log birdhouse   42

Post for birdhouse or feeder   46

Feeder with seed spreader   52

Birdhouse with bevelled roof panels   58

Tools for building birdhouses   63

Index   64

Open-sided feeder (top left), gabled birdhouse (far left), hollow log birdhouse (left)

Sharing your garden with birds

If you want native birds to visit – and enliven – your garden, it is important to provide them with an environment that supplies appropriate food, shelter and nesting sites. Birdhouses and feeders must be carefully planned and maintained.

PLANNING A BIRDHOUSE OR FEEDER

Britain's native birds include a variety of thrushes, tits, warblers and finches. In order to survive successfully in the wild, these species need trees, flowers and shrubs that provide them with fruits, seeds, insects and shelter. The natural habitat for many of these birds is deciduous woodland.

In recent years, many of these species of birds have adapted their territorial habits to include visiting the parks and gardens created by the spread of human habitation. Many people like to believe that for this reason it is important to provide birdhouses (also called nest boxes) and feeders in our gardens. However, these structures must be carefully planned and monitored – and, as importantly, impeccably maintained – if they are going to be of benefit to native birds.

Before deciding on the site and style of your birdhouse or feeder, spend some time investigating your neighbourhood and your own garden. Find out what types of birds visit your local area – there are many books available to help you identify the different species. If possible, take a few weeks to study the habits of visiting birds. Try to find out what they may be feeding on: are they fruit-eaters or seed-eaters, or do they scavenge for insects? Check for nests in the garden, without disturbing them, and take note of the height at which they are built.

BIRD-FRIENDLY GARDENS

The best way to attract birds to your garden (and provide them with a constant food supply) is to include a variety of trees, shrubs and other plants – particularly native plants – in your garden. Gardens planted with roses, azaleas and gardenias may look attractive and smell nice, but they do not contain the diversity required to support a healthy ecosystem.

To encourage seed-eaters, plant seed-bearing plants such as lavender, sunflower and teasel. Birch, as well as beech, is a good seed-bearing tree – plant these to attract finches. Birds such as thrushes love berries and fruit – suitable fruit- or berry-bearing plants include the rowan, cotoneaster and hawthorn.

Many birds feast on spiders and aphids, thereby acting as a form of natural insect control. Avoid using

If you decide to provide supplementary food, it is important to find out what food is the correct one for the particular bird species in your garden. This practical and economical feeder dispenses the seed by means of a seed spreader.

pesticides wherever possible; if you feel that you must, apply a pyrethrum-based spray sparingly.

A large number of British birds live close to, and feed on the ground, making good use of the natural cover and shelter offered by logs, thick grass and shrubs. Brambles and climbers such as honeysuckle provide good cover.

SUPPLEMENTARY FEEDING

If the food-bearing plants in your garden haven't reached a stage where they are attracting birds yet, then providing supplementary food for the birds is an option.

Many wildlife experts object to the idea of supplementary feeding, based on the idea that a constant supply of artificial food makes birds dependent and lazy, and increases the risk of predation by larger animals and other birds.

Supplementary feeding may cause dietary problems, and could increase the risk of disease because of the concentration of birds around a particular feeding point. Aggressive species such as the magpie and crow, and even sparrows and starlings, are encouraged into gardens by feeders, often at the expense of other, less aggressive, birds.

BIRDHOUSE SIZES*

BIRD TYPE	BIRDHOUSE DIMENSIONS
Blue tit	150 x 150 x 250 mm high
Coal tit	150 x 150 x 250 mm high
Great tit	150 x 150 x 250 mm high
Nuthatch	150 x 150 x 250 mm high
House sparrow	150 x 150 x 250 mm high
Robin	150 x 150 x 250 mm high
Pied wagtail	150 x 150 x 250 mm high
Wren	150 x 150 x 250 mm high
Spotted flycatcher	150 x 150 x 250 mm high
Great spotted woodpecker	140 x 140 x 400 mm high

*Information supplied by John Day at the Royal Society for the Protection of Birds, The Lodge, Sandy, Bedfordshire SG19 2DL. See also *Nestboxes* by Chris de Feu, British Trust for Ornithology Guide 23.

Research and carefully consider both pro- and anti-feeding arguments before deciding to provide a bird feeder.

If you want to feed the birds, a mixture of foods and seed is recommended – make sure you use the right seed mix for the species in your area. Your local aviary supply shop can often give you advice on the use of vitamin supplements and the right seed choices.

Fresh kitchen scraps such as apple cores and vegetable peelings can be given as a dietary supplement. Magpies don't mind the occasional piece of meat and cheese. Give only small amounts of food that will be quickly eaten up, and do not feed birds every day. In spring and

ENTRANCE DIAMETER	HEIGHT ABOVE GROUND
25 mm (minimum)	2.5 m
25 mm (minimum)	2.5 m
28 mm (minimum)	2.5 m
32 mm (minimum)	2.5 m
32 mm (minimum)	2.5 m
cut front in half	2.5 m
cut front in half	2.5 m
cut front in half	2.5 m
cut front in half	2.5 m
50 mm (minimum)	3 m

summer, a time when birds rest more often, reduce the amount provided.

You must keep the bird feeder spotlessly clean to prevent the spread of disease. Uneaten and spilled food left on or near the feeder will also attract vermin and other pests.

A permanent, reliable source of clean water is just as important in attracting birds to the garden as a supply of food and a sheltered habitat. Any birdbath or bowl of water to be used by birds should have sloping sides and must be no more than 5 cm deep.

DESIGNING AND SITING A BIRDHOUSE

The best time to install birdhouses is in winter, before the breeding season begins. Birdhouses should be situated in quiet, well-protected areas, sheltered from the wind, out of direct summer sun and attached firmly to their support. (On pages 46–51 you will find directions for

These birdhouses, made in traditional 'folk art' style, are meant for use as interior decoration only.

Birdhouses that are particularly deep should have a piece of wire mesh attached to the inside face leading up to the entrance hole, to help the fledgling birds climb out. Alternatively, you can use saw cuts to form a type of 'ladder' on the inner face of the birdhouse.

The designs in this book can be modified to suit the requirements of many different native birds. Refer to the table on page 6 for information about building a suitable birdhouse for the species you want to attract – further information can be obtained from the Royal Society for the Protection of Birds and the British Trust for Ornithology. For advice on what materials to use, see page 64.

building a post that will suit most types of birdhouses and feeders.)

If you are using a wooden pole, make sure it has a smooth surface, and don't place it adjacent to fences or trees that a cat can climb in order to reach the birdhouse. A galvanised water pipe also makes a good pole. If you place the birdhouse in a tree, be sure to cat-proof the tree: a galvanised sheet metal collar can be wrapped around the trunk to prevent animals from climbing up it (a collar can also be fitted to a wooden pole).

If you are fixing the birdhouse to a wall, use suitable brackets and anchors. The table on page 6 will help you place the birdhouse at a height from the ground that is most suitable for the types of birds you want to attract.

HOLLOW LOGS

Hollow logs provide ideal nesting sites for some bird species. They can look attractive in a garden and will provide shelter for many of the animals upon which birds love to feed, such as insects.

Do not remove logs from woodland sites in order to relocate them in your garden. This upsets the natural balance of forests and woodland, as it deprives many birds, insects and animals of their habitat. An arboriculturist should be able to supply you with an offcut from a tree with a decayed heart.

BIRDHOUSE MAINTENANCE

Keep the birdhouse relatively clean. It is a good idea to place a couple of handfuls of wood shavings or sawdust at the bottom to help with moisture control. Many designs in this book include hinged lids or removable bases to make cleaning easier. After every breeding season, when the fledgling birds have left, inspect the inside of the birdhouse and clean out any unwanted pests and insects.

Most nests can be removed after each breeding season, as many birds will not build on top of old nests or use the same nest twice. Even so, you should find out about the nesting habits of the particular bird species before removing nests. Use warm water and a mild detergent to clean inside the birdhouse. Wiping out the birdhouse with a cloth soaked in disinfectant will keep most bird parasites under control.

The most important thing is to enjoy the birds in your garden. Watch them flutter among the trees and bushes, and listen to their songs. You will learn much about the unique wildlife around you and come to better understand your own relationship with the environment.

DECORATIVE BIRDHOUSES

Birdhouses also have a place indoors as quaint decorative items. Without the constraint of providing the correct habitat for a specific bird, you can let your imagination run free and create houses of any shape, colour or size. Design ideas include birdhouses with steep-pitched shingled roofs, spires, front fences and several rooms, as shown on these facing pages.

Basic carpentry skills and lots of imagination are all you require to build a purely decorative birdhouse. A functional birdhouse for the garden must be specially designed and built with the needs of the feathered residents in mind.

Hanging birdhouse

This diamond-shaped birdhouse is designed to be suspended from a tree or from a tall garden structure such as a pergola. An optional false floor can be fitted inside the birdhouse to provide a flat, stable surface for nesting birds.

TOOLS

- Combination square
- Pencil
- Measuring tape or fold-out rule
- Utility knife
- Jigsaw (or portable circular saw, tenon saw or crosscut saw)
- Smoothing plane
- Hammer
- Vice
- Electric drill
- Drill bits: 3 mm, 5 mm, 8 mm, countersink; 50 mm hole saw
- Screwdriver (cross-head or slotted)
- Nail punch
- Cork sanding block or electric sander

CUTTING OUT

1 The material should already have surfaces dressed square and smooth. Check that the edges are straight and square. If necessary, plane one edge.

2 Use the combination square and pencil to set out the parts along the timber. Leave a 5 mm space between each part to allow for saw cuts and planing back. Once you are satisfied that the sizes are correct, square the lines around the timber with a pencil. Use a combination square and utility knife to score over the lines to cut the cross-grain fibres.

3 Use a jigsaw (or alternative saw) to cut the components to rough sizes. Temporarily nail the front and back

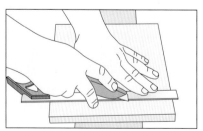

2 Set out the parts on the timber. Use a utility knife to score over the lines to cut the cross-grain fibres.

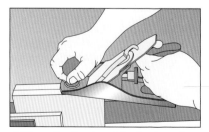

3 Place the front and back pieces in a vice and plane them to the marked lines. Make sure the edges are square.

This birdhouse was built with durable Western red cedar, which will mellow with age to an attractive silver shade. The timber was finished with two coats of vegetable oil – the oil should be reapplied once every four to six months.

MATERIALS★

Part	Material	Length	No.
Front/back	225 x 25 mm timber PAR	200 mm	2
Side	175 x 25 mm timber PAR	181 mm	1
Side	175 x 25 mm timber PAR	200 mm	1
Roof panel	250 x 25 mm timber PAR	254 mm	1
Roof panel	250 x 25 mm timber PAR	235 mm	1
Lipping	50 x 25 mm timber PAR	235 mm	2
Lipping	50 x 25 mm timber PAR	270 mm	2
False floor (optional)	150 x 25 mm timber PAR	142 mm	1

OTHER: Two 30 mm nails; eighteen 40 mm nails; six 35 mm x 8 gauge brass countersunk screws; epoxy resin adhesive; water-based wood filler; one 38 x 8 mm timber dowel; one sheet of 180 grit abrasive paper; vegetable oil (or 250 ml clear acrylic varnish); 6 mm sash cord

★ Finished size: 258 mm long; 380 mm wide; 330 mm tall. Timber sizes given here are nominal. For timber types and sizes see page 64.

pieces together using two 30 mm nails, then place the pieces in a vice and plane them to the marked lines. The finished width will be 200 mm. Make sure the edges are square.

4 Following step 3, bring all the remaining components to the correct lengths specified in the instructions and in the diagram on page 13.

5 Take the front and back pieces and mark the bottom corner with a cross. Measure out 70 mm each way from the marked bottom corner – this measurement is for the two screws seen on the front and back. At the 70 mm points, drill a 5 mm hole 9 mm in from the edge, then countersink the holes.

6 Take the 181 mm long side piece and cut and plane it to a width of 142 mm. Next, take the 200 mm long side piece and cut and plane it to a width of 142 mm. Mix a small amount of epoxy resin adhesive and apply a little to the short edge. Start two 40 mm nails 9 mm in from the edge and about 25 mm in from each side. Bring the two side pieces together to form a 200 x 200 mm right angle, then finish nailing the pieces together.

7 Separate the two nailed front and back pieces. Apply some adhesive to the edges of the right-angled piece and place the front piece in position, aligning it with the sides. Fix the front piece with a 40 mm nail near

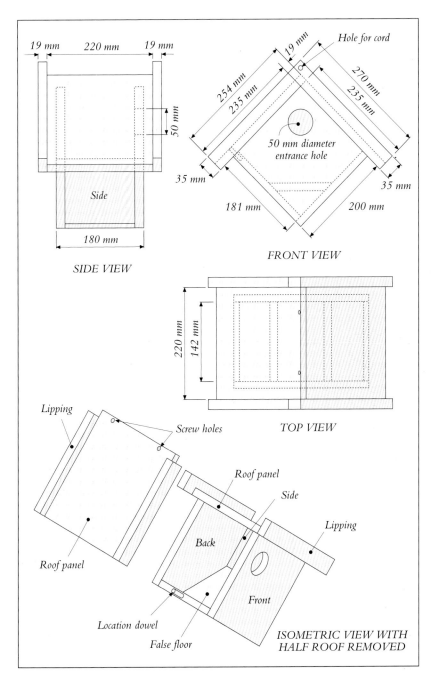

19 mm   220 mm   19 mm

50 mm

Side

180 mm

SIDE VIEW

19 mm   Hole for cord

254 mm
235 mm

270 mm
235 mm

50 mm diameter
entrance hole

35 mm   35 mm

181 mm   200 mm

FRONT VIEW

220 mm   142 mm

TOP VIEW

Lipping

Screw holes

Roof panel

Side

Roof panel

Lipping

Back

Front

Location dowel

False floor

**ISOMETRIC VIEW WITH
HALF ROOF REMOVED**

the outer end. Use two 35 mm
screws to complete the attachment of
the front piece. Repeat for the back
piece, to create a basic box shape.

ADDING THE ROOF

8 Turn the box so that it sits on the
workbench with its roofless top face
upwards. Apply a little adhesive to
the three exposed edges. Place the
235 mm long roof panel flush with
the top edges of the box, ensuring
there is a 20 mm overhang at each
side. Fix this panel to the box using
three 40 mm nails, one in the front
piece, one in the back and one in the
side piece.

9 Turn the box over so the open
side faces up. To insert the dowel,

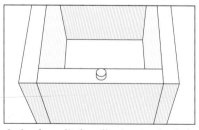

*9 Apply a little adhesive to the hole
in the box only, and insert the 38 x
8 mm dowel.*

first locate the centre of the side
piece along the top edge and drill an
8 mm hole to a depth of 30 mm.
Take the 254 mm roof panel and lay
it in position on the box. Along the
top edge, measure in 50 mm from
each side and 9 mm in from the edge
for the screw holes. Drill a 5 mm
hole at each point and countersink
the holes. On the underside, mark
the position for the dowel hole and
drill an 8 mm hole to a depth of 10
mm. Apply a little adhesive to the
dowel hole in the box only, and then
insert the 38 x 8 mm dowel. Do not
apply any of the adhesive to the hole
in the roof panel.

10 Fit the roof panel in position and
fasten it down with two 35 mm brass
screws. Do not use adhesive – you
will need to remove this roof panel
later in order to insert the false floor
(step 17) and to clean the birdhouse.

11 Lay the box face upwards and
apply a little adhesive to the front
edge of the removable roof panel.
Take a 235 mm long lipping, which
should be cut to a width of 35 mm,
and attach it to the roof panel. Keep
it flush with the inner face and outer
edge of the roof. Use 40 mm nails to
fasten the lipping, which should be
flush with the upper edge of the
roof. Apply some adhesive to the
other edge of the box and attach a
270 mm long lipping (which should
be cut to a width of 35 mm). Turn
the box over and repeat the process
for the lippings on the opposite side.

12 With a combination square, measure vertically upwards 215 mm from the bottom apex of the box, then mark the position. Use a 50 mm hole saw to make the entrance hole in the front of the birdhouse.

FINISHING THE BIRDHOUSE

13 Use a combination square to mark vertical lines 14 mm down from the top apex of the lipping. Mark these lines on both the front and back of the box. Drill an 8 mm hole at these positions.

14 Punch all the nails below the surface and fill them with wood filler. Sand the unit well with 180 grit abrasive paper, working in the direction of the grain.

15 This birdhouse is finished with two coats of vegetable oil applied with a pad of steel wool soaked in the oil. Wipe off any excess with a clean, dry cloth. Leave the birdhouse for a few days to allow the oil to soak into the timber before applying a second coat of oil.

16 To finish, pass a piece of 6 mm sash cord through the holes and secure with a 'figure 8' knot. The birdhouse is now ready to hang. You may also want to fit a false floor in the birdhouse at this point.

ADDING A FALSE FLOOR

17 A false floor can be inserted in the birdhouse to give the birds a more stable and even place to nest.

FINISHING PRODUCTS

Water-based finishing products have been used in the projects in this book wherever possible. When oil is used, vegetable oil is recommended, rather than some of the commercially available finishing oils such as teak oil or Danish oil. Vegetable cooking oils are a good substitute, but may not protect the timber for as long. Even so, they won't damage the birds' health, and they are kept in most kitchens.

Water-based acrylic paints are recommended, as they outperform oil-based paints. Avoid the use of glossy paints, as they do not seem to be as attractive to birds as the matt or low-sheen types.

This false floor simply rests inside the birdhouse and is not nailed in place. Don't insert it until after you have sanded, stained and found a position for the birdhouse. Take the 142 mm long timber for the false floor and cut it to 125 mm wide. Use a smoothing plane to bevel the two long edges to 45 degrees, so that the floor sits neatly in the base of the birdhouse.

18 Drill four or five drainage holes in the false floor, unscrew the roof panel as discussed in step 10, and insert the false floor. If you want, you could also drill drainage holes in the bottom apex of the birdhouse.

Open-sided feeder

The design of this charming feeder is simple but effective. The roof, which is bevelled and planed to a pitched shape, keeps the seed dry. Raised side rails prevent any food from falling out.

MATERIALS*			
PART	MATERIAL	LENGTH	NO.
Side rail	50 x 16 mm timber PAR	255 mm	4
Post	25 x 25 mm timber PAR	165 mm	4
Base	225 x 16 mm timber PAR	193 mm	1
Roof	75 x 75 mm timber PAR	300 mm	3

OTHER: Four 20 mm panel pins; four brass cup hooks; four 38 x 8 mm timber dowels; masking tape; epoxy resin adhesive; water-based wood filler; abrasive paper: one sheet of 100 grit and one sheet of 180 grit; 250 ml exterior acrylic paint of your choice; required length of brass chain

*Finished size: 290 mm long (roof); 290 mm wide (roof); 240 mm tall (from base of feeder to top of roof). Timber sizes are nominal. For timber types and sizes see page 64.

CUTTING OUT

1 Take the 225 x 16 mm timber for the base, and using a combination square set at 193 mm and a pencil, mark a line along the length of the board. Use a power saw or tenon saw to cut the piece close to this width. Square a line near one end of the timber and mark off the length to 193 mm. Square all lines over the edges and across the faces. Cut the piece to length.

2 Take the 50 x 16 mm material for the side rails and mark off four rails 255 mm long, leaving 5 mm spaces between each of them to allow for saw cuts. Cut the side rail pieces slightly over-length.

3 Measure in 19 mm from each end of the side rails, mark with a pencil, then square a line across one top edge and over the sides to half the width. Use a piece of scrap timber to mark the 12 mm wide halving joint. Hold the material so that it nearly covers the line, and mark the thickness on the other side. Square this line across the edge and over the face to about halfway down. With a utility knife, trace over the marked

This feeder is suspended from weather-resistant brass chains, but it can also be mounted on a post – at least 2 m above the ground – as a 'bird table'. Feeders should be placed in a sheltered location within a short flying distance of cover.

TOOLS

- Combination square
- Pencil
- Measuring tape or fold-out rule
- Utility knife
- Marking gauge
- Safety glasses
- Jigsaw
- Tenon saw
- Portable circular saw
- Portable power plane or smoothing plane
- Cork sanding block or electric sander
- Vice
- Two 300 mm quick-action cramps or two sash or adjustable cramps
- Chisel: 12 mm
- Sawhorse (optional)
- Hammer
- Electric drill
- Drill bit: 8 mm
- Sliding bevel
- Nail punch

lines in order to cut the surface fibres. Mark the waste area.

4 Use a combination square to mark a depth of 20.5 mm for the halving joints on each face. Clamp all four pieces in a vice or cramp and use a tenon saw to cut on the waste side of each line to the depth mark. Use the 12 mm chisel to remove the waste from the joint. The joints should fit snugly, but not too tightly. Measure

the diagonal distances to check that the frame will be square.

ASSEMBLING THE FRAME, POSTS AND BASE

5 Mix a little adhesive and assemble the frame on a flat surface. Use scrap material and 20 mm panel pins to temporarily brace the frame diagonally, then leave to dry.

6 While the assembled frame is drying, use a smoothing plane to bring the base piece to fit neatly in the frame. When planing the end grain, always plane from the outer edges towards the centre to avoid chipping the timber.

7 On the 25 x 25 mm timber, mark off four posts each 165 mm long. Cut the posts with a tenon saw. Place all four pieces end upwards in a vice and mark the centre of each end. With an 8 mm drill bit, drill a 29 mm deep dowel hole.

8 Mix some adhesive and then apply it sparingly to the edges of the base piece. Insert the base in the frame,

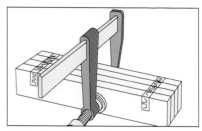

4 Mark a depth of 20.5 mm for the halving joints on each face. Clamp all four pieces.

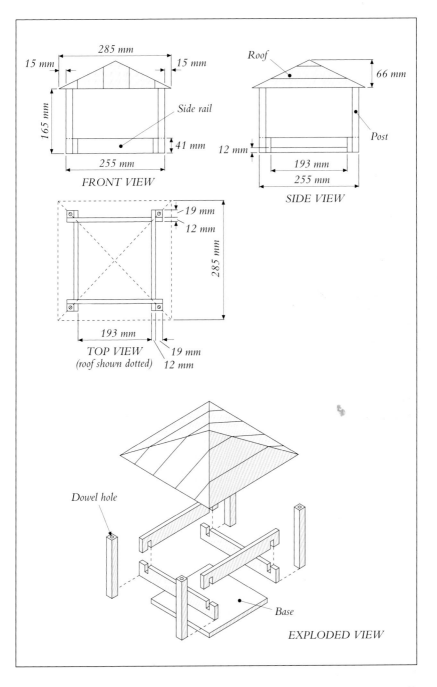

FRONT VIEW

285 mm
15 mm
15 mm
165 mm
Side rail
41 mm
255 mm

SIDE VIEW

Roof
66 mm
Post
12 mm
193 mm
255 mm

TOP VIEW
(roof shown dotted)

19 mm
12 mm
285 mm
193 mm
19 mm
12 mm

Dowel hole

Base

EXPLODED VIEW

flush with the bottom of the frame. Use a 20 mm panel pin in the centre of each side to fasten the base.

9 Place adhesive in the outside corners of the frame and tape the posts in position with dowel holes at the top. Use a square to check the posts are square. Leave to dry.

MAKING THE ROOF PIECES

10 Cut the 75 x 75 mm timber for the roof into three pieces 300 mm in length. Use a combination square and pencil to mark a centre line down the length of one face. On scrap board, mark out the roof pitch: 66 mm high and half the roof width (142.5 mm). Set up a sliding bevel to this pitch. Transfer the angle to the ends of the piece marked with the centre line.

11 Lay the centre piece down flat and place the other two pieces on either side of it. Mark the position where they meet the roof bevel. Use the sliding bevel to transfer the roof bevel to these two pieces so that the slope continues. Mark the waste side.

12 Use a portable power plane or the smoothing plane to plane the roof bevel on the centre piece.

13 Set the foot of the portable circular saw to the angle of the roof bevel. Secure the second piece to a suitable work surface, such as a saw-horse with stops on one side and at the end. Set the depth of the blade so it only just passes through the timber, then cut on the waste side of the line. Repeat this step for the third piece of timber. The waste pieces will be turned over and used for the two outer pieces. (If you cannot cut the full depth with the power saw, turn the material over and cut carefully from the other side on the waste side of the line.)

ASSEMBLING THE ROOF

14 Hold all the roof pieces together and check the fit of the joints. Plane to adjust if necessary. Mix some adhesive and apply to each joining face, then rub the joints together so a little adhesive squeezes out. Repeat this process until all five pieces that make up the roof have been glued.

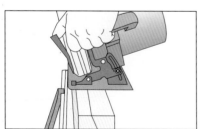

13 Set the foot of the circular saw to the angle of the roof bevel. Cut on the waste side of the line.

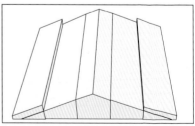

14 Hold all the roof pieces together and check the fit of the joints. Plane to adjust if necessary.

Lay the glued pieces down flat and then leave them to dry completely.

15 When the roof is dry, use an electric plane to remove some of the waste material. When using the electric plane, wear safety glasses, and keep the waste chute pointing away from your face. Mark the centre of the ridge and square a line down the roof and over the bottom face. Square a line down to the bottom at each end and join the points along the bottom. Using these centre lines, mark out the roof size on the underside of the roof. Before cutting, you should check that the roof shape is square by measuring the diagonal distances.

16 Use a jigsaw to cut out the square shape of the roof from the underside. Cut out the shape on the waste side of the line. Turn the roof over and use a straight edge to draw lines from the centre of the apex to the outer corners (these will serve as guide lines for planing across the grain).

17 Secure the roof to a flat surface, with one edge overhanging. Nail timber stops to the work surface as a jig, so the roof won't move as you plane. Plane along the length of the grain first, to within 1–2 mm of the roof bevel. Use a smoothing plane to finish the bevel, keeping the edge of the roof about 2 mm thick.

18 Turn the roof panel around in the jig. Using the electric plane, slowly remove most of the waste from the remaining side of the roof. Remove the last lot of material with the smoothing plane.

FINISHING THE FEEDER

19 Measure the centre-to-centre distance on the posts and transfer the measurements to the underside of the roof. On the roof, drill 8 mm holes 9 mm deep at the marked dowel centre positions. Check the fit of the roof, then mix some adhesive and glue the holes. Press the roof into place and leave it to dry overnight.

20 Punch in all nail holes and fill gaps with wood filler. Use 100 grit abrasive paper to sand the roof, then finish the entire feeder with 180 grit abrasive paper.

21 Apply a coat of paint to the body of the feeder and use a clear acrylic finish for the roof. For the best finish, apply three coats and sand well between each coat. A regular coat of clear finish should be applied to the roof every four to six month to keep it looking at its best.

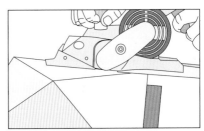

18 Using the electric plane, slowly remove most of the waste from the remaining side of the roof.

This birdhouse was painted in two different colours and then 'distressed' for a rustic effect. The pull-out tray has a brass knob: all fittings on outdoor projects should be brass or stainless steel, which won't corrode as quickly as mild steel.

Gabled birdhouse

This quaint plywood birdhouse features a gabled roof and entrance, as well as a false front door and a pull-out tray.

CUTTING OUT

1 Ensure the plywood is square and the edges are straight. Use a pencil and combination square to mark out the parts, leaving a 5 mm space between each to allow for saw cuts. For the front and back pieces to be easily identified, you need to work from a common line.

2 Score any cross-grain lines on the face side with a utility knife. When parts are set out at the correct size, cut them out with a circular saw, cutting on the waste side of the line.

3 On the front and back pieces use the combination square to continue the drawn lines over the edges and over to the back side. Align the marks on the edges of the two pieces and keep the common edges flush. Nail the front and back together with two 25 mm panel pins and place in a vice. Plane to 170 mm wide and square up the bottom edges. The pieces can be left a little long.

4 On the front piece, use a marking gauge to mark a centre line along the length of the panel and over the edges to the other side. From the centre line, measure up from the bottom 245 mm and 270 mm and

mark these points. From these marks, use the combination square to mark the 45 degree lines of the gable

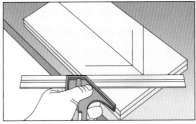

4 Measure up 245 mm and 270 mm. Use the combination square to mark the 45 degree lines of the gable shape.

MATERIALS★

Part	Material	Finished length	Width	No.
Front/back	18 mm A-grade plywood	270 mm	170 mm	2
Side	18 mm A-grade plywood	184 mm	132 mm	1
Side	18 mm A-grade plywood	90 mm	132 mm	1
Tray front	18 mm A-grade plywood	88 mm	130 mm	1
Tray bottom	6 mm A-grade plywood	149 mm	130 mm	1
Base	18 mm A-grade plywood	210 mm	210 mm	1
Roof panel	18 mm A-grade plywood	230 mm	167 mm	1
Roof panel	18 mm A-grade plywood	230 mm	185 mm	1
Entry gable	18 mm A-grade plywood	90 mm	40 mm	1
Entry gable	18 mm A-grade plywood	72 mm	40 mm	1
Tray runner	16 x 16 mm timber PAR	133 mm		2
False door	75 x 16 mm timber PAR	100 mm		1

OTHER: Four 25 mm panel pins; four 15 mm panel pins; twenty-three 40 mm nails; roll of 19 mm masking tape; epoxy resin adhesive; wood filler; abrasive paper: one sheet of 180 grit and one sheet of 240 grit; 250 ml exterior acrylic paint of your choice; small brass knob

★ Finished size: 210 mm long (base); 265 mm wide (roof); 320 mm high. Timber sizes given are nominal. For timber types and sizes see page 64.

shape. Measure up 170 mm from the bottom and mark the entrance hole.

5 Use the utility knife to cut across the grain of the front and back pieces on the top gable only. Clamp the parts to the bench. Cut the pieces with a jigsaw and then smooth them back to the marked lines with a smoothing plane.

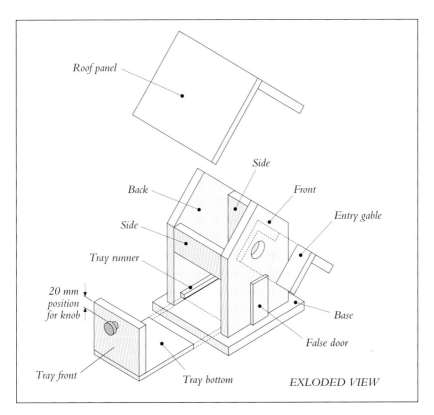

Roof panel

Side

Back

Front

Side

Entry gable

Tray runner

20 mm
position
for knob

Base

False door

Tray front

Tray bottom

EXLODED VIEW

6 Use the smoothing plane to bring all the other pieces back to their given dimensions. Check regularly as you plane that the edges are square and straight.

MAKING TRAY RUNNERS

7 Take the timber for the tray runners and use the smoothing plane to plane a face side and edge square and straight. Set a marking gauge to 10 mm and mark along the face and edge. Clamp the timber to the bench and use a jigsaw to cut on the waste side of the line. Smooth any rough edges, then cut the runners to length.

8 Separate the nailed front and back pieces. Mark up 6 mm from the bottom edge on the inside face of both front and back pieces and then square a line across using the

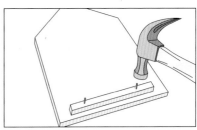

8 Attach the runners to the inside face of the front and back pieces using two panel pins on each runner.

25

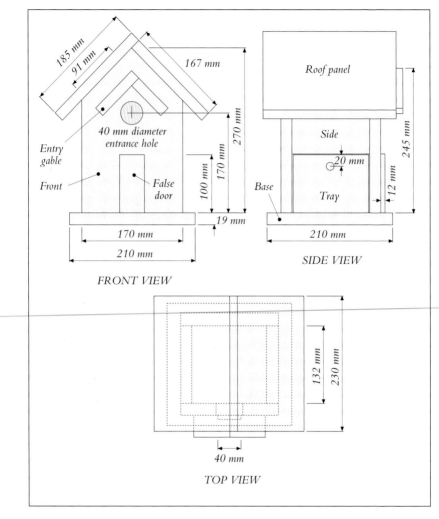

185 mm

91 mm

167 mm

40 mm diameter
entrance hole

Entry
gable

Front

False
door

270 mm

170 mm

100 mm

19 mm

170 mm

210 mm

FRONT VIEW

Roof panel

Side

Base

Tray

20 mm

245 mm

12 mm

210 mm

SIDE VIEW

132 mm

230 mm

40 mm

TOP VIEW

combination square. Measure in 19 mm from the edge of each piece and mark the position. Apply some adhesive to the face of the runners. Attach the runners to the front and back pieces, placing them slightly above the line and between the 19 mm marks. Use two 15 mm panel pins on each runner.

ASSEMBLING THE MAIN UNIT, GABLES AND TRAY

9 Nail the front and back pieces to the side pieces to form a box shape. Fasten each joint using adhesive as well as two 40 mm nails. Keep the edges flush and the top edge of the sides set about 1 mm below the gable intersection.

10 Glue and nail the entry gable pieces together and leave to dry. Glue the tray front and bottom pieces together and nail with two 25 mm panel pins.

11 Glue and nail the base to the box. The base must extend 20 mm equally around all sides. Use 40 mm nails, two into each front and back piece, and one into each side piece.

12 Apply some adhesive to the gable-shaped edge of the front and back pieces. Nail on the 167 mm wide roof panel, using two 40 mm nails – there must be an overhang of 20 mm at the front and back. Make sure the top edge is flush with the top of the gable-shaped edge. Repeat the step for the other roof panel.

MAKING THE FALSE DOOR AND THE ENTRANCE HOLE

13 Cut the false door timber to 40 mm wide x 12 mm thick. Smooth with a plane or abrasive paper. Apply some adhesive, centre the door on the front of the box and secure with tape until the adhesive dries.

14 Fit the tray into its recess – it should slide smoothly. If not, use the smoothing plane to ease the top edges of the tray, and apply candle wax or soap to help it slide. Draw up a centre line and fit a brass knob to the tray, positioning it 20 mm down from the top.

15 Drill the entrance hole in the front of the box using a 40 mm hole saw. Sand the hole smooth inside and out. Fix the entry gable in position with adhesive and hold it in place with masking tape until the adhesive has dried. Allow to dry overnight.

FINISHING

16 Punch all nails below the surface and fill all holes and any gaps. Leave the putty to dry before sanding with 180 grit abrasive paper.

17 Apply the first coat of paint. Allow the paint to dry, then sand back with 180 grit abrasive paper. Apply the second coat, leave to dry, and then sand it back with 240 grit abrasive paper. To finish, apply a third coat of paint.

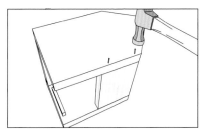

9 Nail front and back pieces to the sides. Keep the top edge of the sides 1 mm below the gable intersection.

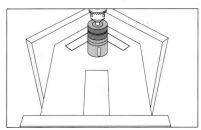

15 Drill the entrance hole in the front of the box using a 40 mm hole saw at the marked position.

Birdhouse with hinged lid

A two-tiered lid made of splayed weatherboard allows access for cleaning. It is secured with a gripper catch to deter predators.

CUTTING OUT

1 Take the timber for the two sides and mark them out to length. Use a 60/30 degree set square to set the sliding bevel to 60 degrees. The 60 degree angles on the sides can be opposed to each other to save timber and time – leave a 5 mm space between the lines for saw cuts. Use the combination square to square the lines over the edge. Then draw a 60 degree line across the back face. Check that the lines match up all around before scoring them with a utility knife to cut the cross-grain fibres. Use the jigsaw to cut the parts close to length and to cut across the marked 60 degree angles.

2 Use two 25 mm panel pins to nail the side pieces together. Place the side pieces in a vice and plane the bottom ends square and straight using

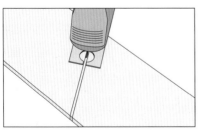

1 Use the jigsaw to cut across the marked 60 degree angles on the side pieces.

the smoothing plane. Turn the pieces around and angle them in the vice so you plane flat. Plane the 60 degree angle back to the line, working from the bottom towards the top to avoid chipping the timber.

3 Take the timber for the front and back pieces and mark off the length.

Wire mesh reaching from the floor to the entrance hole inside this deep birdhouse helps young birds climb out. The hole is located near the top to make it harder for predators to attack nestlings and to keep the nest dark and cool.

MATERIALS★

Part	Material	Length	No.
Side	200 x 25 mm timber PAR	540 mm	2
Front	175 x 25 mm timber PAR	443 mm	1
Back	175 x 25 mm timber PAR	540 mm	1
Base	175 x 25 mm timber PAR	150 mm	1
Lid	6 mm A-grade plywood	244 x 188 mm	1
Roof panel	Splayed weatherboard (timber)	240 x 190 mm	2

OTHER: Two 25 mm panel pins; twenty-two 40 mm nails; two 36 mm brass hinges; six 16 mm x 4 gauge countersunk brass screws; six 19 mm x 4 gauge countersunk screws; four 16 mm x 4 gauge round-head brass screws; epoxy resin adhesive; water-based wood filler; 300 x 120 mm wire mesh (chicken wire); gripper catch or magnetic catch; one sheet of 180 grit abrasive paper; exterior acrylic paint of your choice

★Finished size: 260 mm long (to edge of roof); 240 mm wide (roof); 550 mm tall (from base to top edge of roof). Timber sizes given are nominal. For timber types and sizes see page 64.

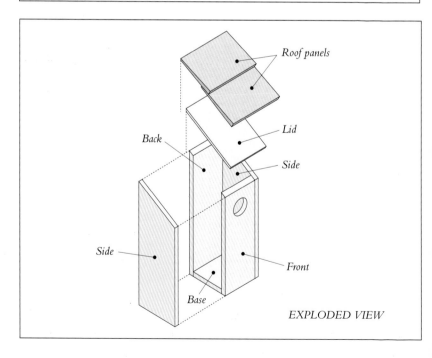

Roof panels

Back

Lid

Side

Side

Front

Base

EXPLODED VIEW

Square the bottom lines across the face and over the edge, and return across the back face. Mark the angled cut on the top end of each piece using the 60 degree angle on the sliding bevel (use the side pieces as a guide to check the lengths). When the pieces have been correctly marked out, use a utility knife to score over the lines.

4 Set the foot of the jigsaw to cut 30 degrees from the vertical. Make the cut on the top of the front and back pieces (on the waste side of the line). Return the foot of the saw to 90 degrees and cut the bottom edge off square on each piece.

5 Align the bottom edge of the front and back pieces, place them in a vice and plane the bottom ends straight and square. Check regularly that you are planing square. Individually turn each piece up in the vice and plane the 60 degree bevel on the top edge. Use the side pieces as a guide to check the lengths.

6 Set the combination square to 150 mm and mark the width along the length of the front and back pieces. Use the jigsaw to cut the pieces to width. Place the two pieces together, with the dressed edges flush in a vice, and plane the sawn edges down to the 150 mm lines.

7 Set out and cut the base piece to 150 x 150 mm. Check diagonal distances to ensure it is square.

ASSEMBLY

8 Mix a little epoxy resin adhesive. Start two 40 mm nails near the bottom edge of the front and back pieces, about 30 mm in from each edge and 9 mm up from the bottom on the face side. Place the base piece in a vice and apply some adhesive before positioning the front piece flush with the bottom and edges of the base. Drive in the nails. Repeat the process to attach the back piece.

9 Attach the side pieces using a little adhesive as well as four 40 mm nails along the back edges and three 40 mm nails along the front edges of each side piece. Place a nail in the bottom edge on both side pieces. Ensure the front and back pieces are flush with the side pieces.

MAKING THE LID

10 Take the plywood and mark out and cut a piece for the lid measuring 270 x 188 mm. Use a smoothing plane to bevel one 188 mm long edge to 60 degrees. Measure in 20 mm from the end of the bevelled edge and mark this point. Repeat for

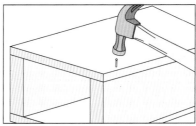

9 Attach the side pieces using four 40 mm nails along the back edges and three 40 mm nails on the front edges.

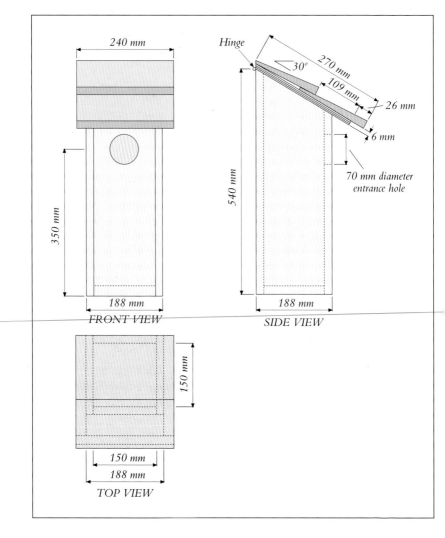

240 mm

Hinge

30°

270 mm

109 mm

26 mm

6 mm

70 mm diameter
entrance hole

540 mm

350 mm

FRONT VIEW

188 mm

SIDE VIEW

188 mm

150 mm

150 mm

188 mm

TOP VIEW

the other side. Hold the hinge edge flush with the mark and, with the knuckle of the hinge against the edge, locate the position of the screw holes. Drill 2 mm pilot holes in the lid. Attach the hinge (temporarily) using two 16 mm x 4 gauge countersunk brass screws. The screws will go through the plywood. Repeat for the other side.

11 Align the lid on the box and drill pilot holes for the other hinge leaves vertically into the box. Attach the lid with six 19 mm x 4 gauge brass countersunk screws. Once the lid

closes properly, remove it, leaving the hinges on the box.

12 Cut the two pieces of splayed weatherboard for the roof panels to a length of 240 mm (the front panel will be attached first). Mix up some epoxy adhesive. Use the combination square to draw a line 26 mm along the thick edge of the splayed board on what will be the back face. Spread adhesive over the back of the weatherboard. Align the lid with the marked line, making sure it is centred, then fasten it to the roof panel with two 25 mm panel pins. Don't drive the pins in all the way, as they will be removed in step 19.

13 Turn the lid over and align the second roof panel so that it comes halfway down the lid. Mark the position. Apply a little adhesive near the top of the lid and position the second roof panel. Hold the panel in place with a heavy object or two G-cramps until the adhesive has set. When the adhesive has set, trim back the panel's overhanging edge flush with the hinging edge of the lid.

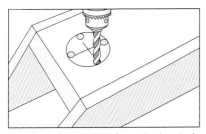

14 Drill four holes through the circle and use a jigsaw to cut out the entrance hole.

FINISHING

14 Find and mark the centre of the front of the birdhouse (along the bottom). Measure up 350 mm and mark the entrance hole position. With a compass, draw a 70 mm diameter circle on the face. Drill four 8 mm holes through the circle and use a jigsaw to cut out the entrance hole. In the base of the box, drill four 5 mm drainage holes.

15 Use a hand stapler to fasten wire mesh to the inner face, stretching from the floor to the entry hole.

16 Attach a strong magnetic catch or gripper catch to one side wall with four 16 mm x 4 gauge round-head screws. Fix the striker to the inside of the lid.

17 Punch all nails below the surface and fill the holes with wood filler. Fill any gaps and leave to dry.

18 Sand the body of the birdhouse using 180 grit abrasive paper. Apply the first of three coats of exterior acrylic paint to the outer surfaces only. When the paint is dry, sand lightly between each coat with 180 grit abrasive paper.

19 Remove the cramps and nails from the lid. Give it a light sand and paint as in step 18, then reattach using all the screws. The birdhouse is now ready to be positioned. Note that it is not suitable for wall mounting, because of its hinged lid.

In a contemporary take on the traditional all-white dovecote, only the basic unit has been painted. The timber roof has been finished in a clear exterior acrylic to emphasize the intricacy of the design.

Dovecote

A dovecote is the ultimate romantic garden feature. This project requires precision and patience, especially in the assembly of the roof, with its overlapping slats and mitred ridge capping.

SIDE ASSEMBLY

1 Use the 60/30 degree set square to tilt the base of the portable power saw to a 60 degree angle. Place the plywood for the sides across the work surface. Set up a straight edge parallel to one long edge, far enough in to cut the angle on the edge of a sheet of plywood. Clamp the straight edge to the board, and make an angled cut along one edge.

2 Cut the next angle in the opposite direction. Turn the plywood over and set the straight edge parallel to the angled edge, at the necessary distance in order to produce a piece that is 310 mm wide. The distance set from the line will be determined by measuring the distance from the inner edge of the saw blade to the outside edge of the foot (cut a piece of scrap material to check). Cut the second side piece.

3 Working from one square end of the plywood, use a combination square and pencil to mark out the length of the first side piece (750 mm) on the inside face. The inside face is the narrow face of the wood. Position a straight edge parallel to the line so that the saw will cut

TOOLS
• Set square: 60/30 degree
• Measuring tape or fold-out rule
• Combination square and pencil
• Two quick-release cramps
• Portable power saw
• Jigsaw or hand saw
• Tenon saw
• Smoothing plane
• Hammer
• Vice
• Compass with extension arm, or protractor
• Two sliding bevels
• Utility knife
• Bench hook
• Side cutters or pliers
• Screwdriver (slotted or cross-head)
• Electric drill
• Drill bits: 3 mm, 5 mm, 8 mm, countersink; 25 mm spade bit or hole saw
• Nail punch
• Cork sanding block or electric sander

under-length on the outside face. Set the saw to a 45 degree angle and carefully make the cut. Square off the end of the plywood before you set out

MATERIALS★				
PART	MATERIAL	LENGTH	WIDTH	NO.
Side	18 mm A-grade plywood	750 mm	310 mm	6
Base	18 mm A-grade plywood	800 mm	800 mm	1
Support bracket	18 mm A-grade plywood	250 mm	250 mm	4
Internal floor	18 mm A-grade plywood	600 mm	600 mm	1
Roof panel	4 mm A-grade plywood	504 mm	420 mm	6
Base lipping	100 x 25 mm timber PAR	440 mm		6
Fascia	75 x 16 mm timber PAR	400 mm		6
Roof slat★★	50 x 10 mm timber wedge	2200 mm		—
Ridge capping★★	12 x 10 mm timber	580 mm		12

OTHER: Four 25 mm panel pins; eighteen 40 mm nails; eighteen 15 mm panel pins; eleven 50 mm x 8 gauge brass countersunk screws; scrap material for perches/supports; masking tape; two pieces of rope 2.4 m long; epoxy resin adhesive; twelve 50 mm wide strips of cotton cloth; paint brush; abrasive paper: one sheet of 120 grit and one sheet of 180 grit; water-based wood filler; 500 ml exterior acrylic paint of your choice; 250 ml clear exterior acrylic finish

★Finished size: 880 mm long; 880 mm wide; 1042 mm tall. Timber sizes given are nominal. For timber types and sizes see page 64.
★★Cut roof slat and ridge capping material from one piece 2400 x 100 x 50 mm timber DAR.

the next side piece. Use the combination square to square the line across the end, and cut with a jigsaw or a hand saw. To finish off, use a smoothing plane to smooth and square

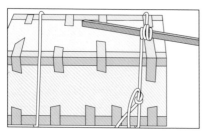

5 Insert a stick through the rope and twist it so that the rope tightens and brings the joints firmly together.

the end. Repeat this process to cut the other five side pieces.

4 Lay the sides down with the outside face upper most, then place them next to one another with the joint edges tightly aligned and the bottom edges flush. Apply one strip of masking tape along the length of each joint, and at least four pieces of tape across. Fold the hexagon up and tape along the remaining joint.

5 Loosely tie the two pieces of rope around the hexagon. Insert a small stick through the rope and twist it so

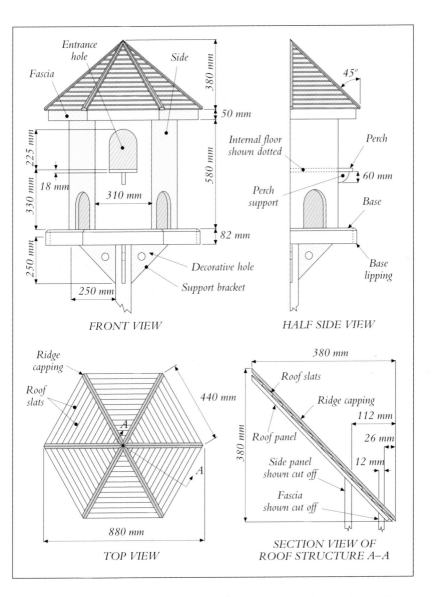

Entrance hole
Side
Fascia

380 mm
50 mm

225 mm
18 mm
310 mm
330 mm

Internal floor shown dotted
Perch
60 mm

Perch support
Base

580 mm
82 mm
250 mm

Base lipping

250 mm

Decorative hole
Support bracket

FRONT VIEW

45°

HALF SIDE VIEW

Ridge capping
Roof slats

440 mm

A
A

380 mm
Roof slats
Ridge capping
112 mm
26 mm
12 mm
Roof panel
Side panel shown cut off
Fascia shown cut off

880 mm

TOP VIEW

SECTION VIEW OF
ROOF STRUCTURE A–A

that the rope tightens and brings the joints firmly together. Ensure the joints come up neatly and the angles are even. Use a smoothing plane to adjust if necessary.

6 Mix adhesive for the joints. Undo the rope and lay the side pieces flat, inside face up. Glue the face of each joint, reassemble the hexagon and tighten the ropes. Allow to dry.

MAIN ROOF ASSEMBLY

7 On the plywood for the roof panels mark a triangle with a base length of 440 mm and with a perpendicular height of 504 mm. Use a jigsaw to cut the shape slightly over-size and a smoothing plane to bring the triangle back to size.

8 Use this triangle as a template for marking out the other five triangles, then cut them out. Nail all triangles together with two 25 mm panel pins, the template piece to the outside. Place the triangles in a vice and plane to the template size. Remove the nails and plane a 15–20 degree bevel on each of the long edges.

9 Lay out the triangles and tape the joints together. Fold the triangles up and tape the final joint to form a neat hexagonal pyramid with the sides sloping in at 45 degrees. Unfold the pyramid, glue each joint, then refold. Place it base upwards, check the shape is even and leave it until dry.

10 Cut six strips of cotton material to the length of each joint. With a paintbrush apply adhesive inside the roof along each side of a joint. Place the cloth strip on top of the adhesive, pushing the cloth into the joint (paint more adhesive over the cloth if needed). Stand the pyramid base downwards to dry.

BASE ASSEMBLY

11 Take the plywood for the base and use a compass with an extension arm

to draw a circle 800 mm in diameter. Without changing the radius, place the point of the compass on the circle and mark off six equal distances around the circle, ending up where you started. Use a straight edge to join the points to form a hexagon. Cut out with a jigsaw and plane back to the lines, keeping the edges straight and square.

12 Set up a sliding bevel to 60 degrees. Hold the timber for the base lippings against one edge of the base and mark off the inside length on the top edge of the timber (400 mm). Mark off the angle to the outside face. Square the lines across each face and use the bevel to return them across the remaining edge (they should meet up). Number the lipping corresponding to the edge on the base. Score the lines, then use a tenon saw to cut the mitres on each end. Clean up with a smoothing plane. Repeat for all lippings.

13 Glue the edge of the base and attach one lipping flush with the top of the base, using 40 mm nails – punch the nails below the surface. Repeat for all lippings. Use the smoothing plane to make a 10 mm chamfer around the top edge of the lipping.

FASCIA ASSEMBLY

14 Use the sliding bevel set at 60 degrees to mark a mitre across the edge of the fascia timber, near one end. Measure out 400 mm on the outer face and mark the opposite

mitre on the other end. Mark out five more pieces the same way.

15 Plane the top edge to a 45 degree angle. Use the combination square to check the angle and ensure you are planing parallel to the bottom edge.

16 Trace the mitre lines with a utility knife. With the bottom edge facing up in the bench hook, cut the mitres, keeping the cut square. Insert two 15 mm panel pins in one face of each adjoining mitre and cut the heads off to leave 6–7 mm exposed. Push the mitres together to check the fit. Repeat for all joints. Take the frame apart and glue each joint, then reassemble and leave to dry.

ENTRY HOLES AND PERCHES

17 Mark out entrance holes 225 mm high and 150 mm wide. With an 8 mm bit, drill holes near the bottom corners of the upper entrance holes. Use a jigsaw with a fine-toothed blade to cut the holes, and smooth with 120 grit abrasive paper. Take the waste material, square across, and cut off the curved end of three pieces for the

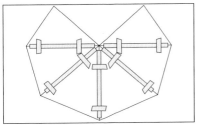

9 Lay out the plywood roof panel triangles and use masking tape to tape the joints.

perches. Use a smoothing plane to dress the square end.

18 Make the internal floor now. Stand the dovecote on the 18 mm plywood and trace the inside shape of the unit. Cut out the shape with a jigsaw. Insert the floor level with the bottom edges of the top entrance holes and fix with six 40 mm nails.

19 Place two 15 mm panel pins 8 mm down from each upper hole, 80 mm apart. Nail in to half their length, then cut off the heads. Push the perches into place. Remove the perches, then glue and reposition them. For the perch supports, mark a 120 mm diameter circle on a waste piece, then quarter it. Cut out with a jigsaw, glue and tape them in place, then leave to dry.

CUTTING ROOF SLATS

20 Set up a marking gauge to 4 mm and mark a line down one wide face of the roof slat timber. Square the line over the ends. Mark a line from the gauged line to the opposite corner on the end of the material: this is the angle of the roof slat. Plane the angle on the edge of the timber.

21 Clamp the roof slat timber to the bench, gauged line upwards. Using a jigsaw, cut a slat 10 mm thick. Plane the edge again to make the angle. Use a marking gauge to mark the line on the face and repeat the cut. Repeat until the 2400 mm piece has been turned into wedge slats.

22 Place the roof 'pyramid' on a flat surface, base down against a stop. Hold a slat up to the base and mark the bottom length. Set the sliding bevel to the ridge angle – hold the base of the bevel against the bottom edge, position the blade to align with the angle and tighten the screw. Transfer the angle to the slat at the length marks. Cut to length and use as a template for the other sides.

23 Tape the first roof slat piece in place. Mark the length of the second row of slats and use the sliding bevel to set the angle. Use this as a template for the second row of slats, then tape the second piece in place. Repeat to cut all the roof slats.

24 Mix some adhesive and apply to one face of the roof. Place the bottom roof slat on the roof, then attach the rest, ensuring that each piece touches the one below. Work on one side at a time until all sides are covered. Allow to dry.

ADDING RIDGE CAPPING

25 Mark a centre line down the face of one side of the roof, from the roof tip to the centre of the base. Place the butt of the sliding bevel in line with the ridge, then align the blade with the centre line and tighten the screw. This angle will be the mitre angle for the ridge capping. Next set a second sliding bevel to the angle used for cutting the ends of the roof slats. This will be the angle of the foot cut for the ridge capping.

26 Take the ridge capping timber, and with a marking gauge mark a line 4 mm wide along the face side. Use a jigsaw to cut to thickness. Plane the edge and repeat the step to cut twelve pieces 600 mm long. Bevel one long edge of each piece to the angle in step 25 and check the edge fit of the pieces on the ridge.

27 Mark the foot cut close to one end of a ridge capping piece. Ensure the bevelled edge will face in the right direction. With a utility knife and the sliding bevel, make the foot cut. Tape the piece in place, with the foot of the ridge capping touching the bench. Repeat for the capping on the opposite side of the same roof panel. Tape in place with the top ends of the two pieces overlapping. Use a pencil to mark the point of overlap on each piece. With the second sliding bevel mark the mitre angle on each piece, then cut the angles with a utility knife. Adjust the bevels, then tape back into place. Use the two cut ridge pieces as guides for the remaining pieces and repeat the process, taping each one

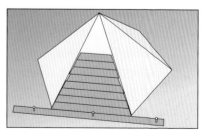

24 Mix some adhesive and apply to one face of the roof. Place the bottom slat on the roof, then attach the rest.

into place. When finished, remove each piece, glue it and tape it back in place (one at a time). Leave to dry.

28 Place the roof on the fascia frame, with an even overhang all round. Turn the roof on to one face to check the bevelled angle of the frame. Glue the bevelled edge of the frame and tape the roof in place. Turn the right way up and leave to dry.

ASSEMBLING THE DOVECOTE

29 Turn the roof upside down and support with packing material. Next, turn the main unit (assembled sides with perches attached) upside down, and locate it evenly within the roof. Trace around the inside of the unit. Remove the unit, apply adhesive to the top edges and relocate it on the roof. Use three strips of cotton cloth wetted with adhesive to join the roof to the main unit. Leave to dry.

30 On the top of the base, draw lines from each corner to the opposite corner. Set the unit on top of the base and align its corners with the marked lines. Ensure the unit is centred, then trace around the outside on to the base. Drill three 5 mm holes through the base, 8 mm inside the traced lines on the sides without low-set entrance holes. Turn the base over and countersink the holes. Position the base over the unit. Drill three 3 mm pilot holes through the 5 mm clearance holes into the unit and use three 50 mm x 8 gauge screws to attach the base.

Nail holes and gaps in the roof have been filled with timber putty that matches the colour of the timber.

MAKING SUPPORT BRACKETS

31 From the plywood cut two squares 250 x 250 mm. Cut them diagonally, then plane smooth. From the square corner, measure in 50 mm and down 130 mm to find the centre of the decorative holes. Use a spade bit or hole saw to cut the holes. In the centre of the base, set out the dimensions of the post (it should be made of 100 x 100 mm timber PAR). Use an offcut from the post to locate brackets centrally on the faces of the post. Drill 5 mm countersunk clearance holes 25 mm in from the ends of the brackets, then fasten the brackets to the bottom of the base with adhesive and four 50 mm screws. Use same-size screws to fix brackets to the post. Concrete the post into the ground, setting it at least 750 mm deep.

32 Fill and sand the dovecote, then apply your chosen finish.

Keep in mind that the twigs or straw you have used on the roof will eventually be broken down by the elements or, most likely, be taken by birds to build their nests. You may need to mend the thatching a couple of times each year.

Hollow log birdhouse

This rustic thatched birdhouse will blend into the general garden scenery. Obtain a log from a sawmill – removing logs from the wild deprives many native animals of their natural habitat.

CUTTING OUT

1 Take the drawing of the birdhouse to a sawmill. Ask the proprietor to use a bandsaw to square up one end of the log and to cut the gable ends on the other end.

2 Wearing protective gardening gloves, use a stiff brush to clean the inside of the log.

3 Turn the log bottom upwards, and support it so it is stable. Set the router to cut a rebate 6 mm deep. Working from the inside of the hollow, run the router in a clockwise direction to remove the waste and create a rebate in the bottom of the log about 12–15 mm wide.

4 Lay the cardboard over the rebated hole. With a pencil, rub over the

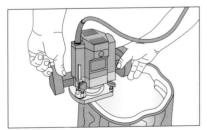

3 Set the router to cut a rebate 6 mm deep. Run the router clockwise to cut a rebate in the bottom of the log.

TOOLS

- Measuring tape or fold-out rule
- Stiff brush
- Gardening gloves
- Electric router
- Router bit: 12 mm
- Jigsaw (or portable circular saw or hand saw)
- Scissors
- Secateurs
- Electric drill
- Drill bits: 2 mm, 3 mm, 4 mm, 5 mm; 50 mm and 35 mm hole saws
- Hammer
- Nail punch
- Screwdriver (cross-head or slotted)
- Smoothing plane
- Hot glue gun
- Blunt-nosed pliers

edge area to create a template of the hole outline. Cut out the template.

5 Lay the template on the plywood for the base and trace around it. Use a jigsaw to cut the base to fit into the rebate. Fasten the base with three 16 mm x 6 gauge brass screws, then drill four 5 mm drainage holes.

MATERIALS*

Part	Material	Finished length	Width	No.
Log	Hollow tree offcut	425 mm	200 mm diam.	1
Roof panel	18 mm A-grade plywood	280 mm	240 mm	1
Roof panel	18 mm A-grade plywood	280 mm	222 mm	1
Base	6 mm A-grade plywood	200 mm	200 mm	1
Roof ridge	Stick	280 mm	20 mm diam.	1

OTHER: Three 16 mm x 6 gauge brass screws; six 40 mm nails; two 35 mm x 8 gauge brass screws; a piece of thin cardboard; crayon or pencil; epoxy resin adhesive; eight hot glue sticks; dried reeds or willow twigs (obtainable from craft stores) or straw; 900 mm copper wire

* Finished size: This will depend on the size of the log obtained. The example shown here is 240 mm in diameter and 450 mm high (from the bottom of the log to the top of the twig roof ridge).

6 Lay the log on the bench and mark positions for a small entrance hole 85 mm from the top and a large hole 130 mm from the bottom. Cut out with 35 mm and 50 mm hole saws.

7 Mark out the plywood for the two roof panels to the sizes given. Use the jigsaw to cut the panels slightly over-size, then plane the edges back to the lines with a smoothing plane, ensuring they are square and straight. Mix some adhesive and apply it to one long edge of the 222 mm wide panel. Use two 40 mm nails to fasten the other roof panel to the first roof panel, making an angle of 90 degrees.

THATCHING THE ROOF
8 Choose several long, straight twigs. Hold them so the ends are roughly flush, then trim the ends with scissors or secateurs. Apply a 20 mm wide layer of hot adhesive at the top and about 200 mm down, and position the twigs on the roof, near one end. Using scrap timber, press the twigs on to the roof until the adhesive begins to set (wear gloves).

9 Repeat until you reach the opposite end, then repeat for the other side. Fill any gaps, and trim the ends of the twigs so they overhang the roof by 40 mm. Attach twigs to the front and rear edges of the roof.

FIXING THE ROOF RIDGE
10 Take the roof ridge stick and drill two 2 mm holes, 20 mm apart and about 50 mm in from each end, right through. Place the end of the wire in

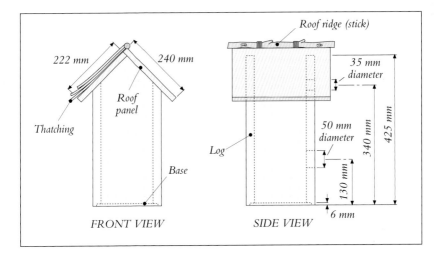

222 mm   240 mm

Roof panel

Thatching

Base

FRONT VIEW

Roof ridge (stick)

35 mm diameter

50 mm diameter

425 mm

340 mm

130 mm

6 mm

Log

SIDE VIEW

one hole and bind it around the stick until you reach the other hole. Push the end of the wire through the second hole. Pull it tight with pliers. Repeat for the other end of the stick. Glue the wire to hold in place.

11 Drill two 3 mm holes in the roof, one on either side near the centre of the ridge. Bind the wire around the middle of the roof ridge stick, then push the ends through the holes on each side of the roof ridge. Turn the roof over and use pliers to pull the

stick tightly to the roof. Twist the wire tight, cut off any excess wire and push the ends out of harm's way.

ATTACHING THE ROOF

12 Find a place on the roof to fasten the two 35 mm x 8 gauge screws that secure the roof to the log. Drill a 5 mm clearance hole through the roof and a 3 mm pilot hole into the log. Glue the gabled end of the log, put the roof on and insert the screws.

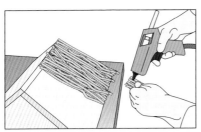

8 Apply a layer of hot adhesive and position the twigs on the roof, near one end.

USING A ROUTER

• Use cramps to secure the work.
• Always do a test cut on a scrap piece to check the settings.
• Wear safety glasses, hearing protection and a dust mask.
• Don't cut to the required size the first time. Always make two or three passes with the router.
• If the router sticks, wipe the fence with soap or candle wax.

Post for birdhouse or feeder

This sturdy, stylish post is designed to be portable, and is anchored in position with steel tent pegs. An optional fixing plate provides an extra-strong fastening for a birdhouse or feeder.

MATERIALS*				
PART	MATERIAL	LENGTH	WIDTH	NO.
Base leg	75 x 38 mm timber PAR	600 mm		2
Pole**	75 x 75 mm timber PAR	2700 mm		1
Brace	75 x 38 mm timber PAR	310 mm		4
Fixing plate (optional)	18 mm A-grade plywood	160 mm	90 mm	1

OTHER: Sixteen 40 mm nails; four 6 x 300–450 mm long steel tent pegs; two 50 mm brass countersunk screws; four 32 mm brass countersunk screws; abrasive paper: one sheet of 120 grit and one sheet of 180 grit; wood filler; epoxy resin adhesive; paintbrush; 500 ml exterior water-based clear finish

* Finished size: 600 mm long (base); 600 mm wide (base); 2.7 m high (will vary). Timber sizes given are nominal. For timber types and sizes see page 64.

** Pole for dovecote (page 34) must be made of 100 x 100 mm timber PAR.

MAKING THE BASE

1 Take the base leg timber and mark out two pieces 600 mm long. Cut to length with a tenon saw, then mark the centre on one face. Measure out 33 mm from one side of centre. Square the line across the face and over each edge, down to half the timber thickness. Place one piece on the marked line on the other piece, and pencil the width of the halving joint. (The post must be modified for use with the dovecote on page 34.)

2 Repeat the step for the other piece, squaring the lines over the

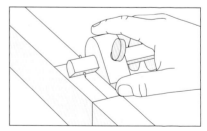

2 Set a marking gauge to half the thickness of the edge. Mark a line between the two pencilled marks.

All edges of the post are chamfered for a finely detailed finish. The Western red cedar timber has been treated with a clear exterior sealer; it should retain its original colour if treated every few months and kept in a shaded position.

47

TOOLS

- Combination square and pencil
- Measuring tape or fold-out rule
- Tenon saw
- Marking gauge
- Utility knife
- G-cramp
- Chisel: 25 mm
- Vice
- Smoothing plane
- Hammer
- Router or spokeshave (optional)
- Sanding cork
- Screwdriver (cross-head or slotted)
- Electric drill
- Drill bits: 3 mm, 5 mm, 8 mm; 25 mm spade bit
- Nail punch

waste. Clamp the timber to the workbench and cut it with the tenon saw on the waste side of the line down to the gauged line. Make a number of cuts in between the lines, about 10 mm apart. Repeat the process for the other half of the base.

4 Use the 25 mm chisel to remove the waste down to the gauged line. Check the depth of the recess as you chisel. Make sure the bottom of the recess is flat, with no high spots (the edge of the chisel makes a useful straight edge). Check the fit and adjust if necessary.

5 With the halving joint assembled, measure in 20 mm from each edge of the joint to form a 26 mm square in the centre of the joint. Do this on both faces of the halving joint. (You can also use a marking gauge set to 20 mm to mark the correct distance in from each edge of the material, on two edges, if you take the joint apart.) Use a pencil to mark the centre of the 26 mm square with a cross. With the joint assembled, use the 25 mm spade bit to drill a hole

edge to halfway down. Set a marking gauge to half the thickness of the timber. On both base leg pieces, mark a line between the two pencilled marks.

3 Use a utility knife to trace the lines for the halving joint, and mark the

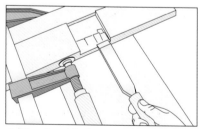

4 Use the chisel to remove the waste down to the gauged line. Check the depth of the recess as you chisel.

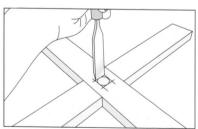

5 Drill a hole through the centre of the assembled joint. Use the chisel to remove any waste from the mortise.

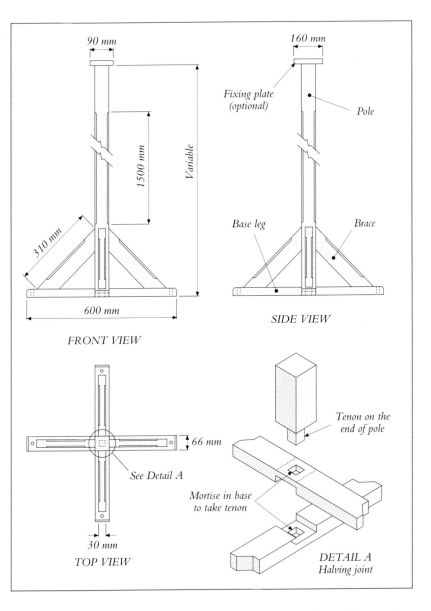

90 mm

160 mm

Fixing plate
(optional)

Pole

1500 mm

Variable

310 mm

Base leg

Brace

600 mm

SIDE VIEW

FRONT VIEW

66 mm

See Detail A

Tenon on the
end of pole

Mortise in base
to take tenon

30 mm

TOP VIEW

DETAIL A
Halving joint

through the centre of the joint – drill
from both sides of the material to be
sure you are drilling straight. Use the
25 mm chisel to remove any

remaining waste from the mortise,
working from both faces towards the
centre to avoid breaking out the
material on the bottom face.

MAKING TENON AND BRACES

6 Make sure the pole is 66 mm square. Use a combination square and pencil to square a line around the timber for the pole, 32 mm up from one end. Set the marking gauge to 20 mm. On the marked end of the pole, working from each face, mark a line across the bottom and down each face to the shoulder line of the tenon. Use the utility knife to trace over the shoulder lines of the tenon.

7 With the pole well supported, use a tenon saw to cut squarely down the shoulder lines on the waste side to the 20 mm marks on each face. Use the chisel to remove the waste from the shoulders of the tenon.

8 Test the fit of the tenon in the mortise. It should be a snug fit, but not too tight. Use the tenon saw to make a diagonal cut down the length of the tenon to accommodate the wedge that will be used to reinforce the joint.

9 Take the timber for the braces and use the combination square set to 45 degrees to mark out the four brace pieces at 310 mm long on their longest edge. It is best to mark them out opposite one another to save some cutting, leaving 5 mm between each piece to allow for the saw cuts. Trace over the lines with the utility knife to cut the cross-grain fibres, then make the mitre cuts with the tenon saw. Hold each piece in a vice and use the smoothing plane to smooth the mitre cuts back to the 45 degree knife lines. Before assembly, sand all the pieces with 120 grit abrasive paper.

10 From a scrap piece of 75 x 38 mm material, cut a fine wedge to fit into the saw cut in the tenon.

11 Mix a little epoxy resin adhesive, apply some to each halving joint and then bring the two halves together. Apply some adhesive to the tenon and the shoulders of the tenon, then fit the base over the tenon, making sure the base sits tightly against the shoulders. Apply a little adhesive to the wedge, insert it in the saw cut and use the hammer to drive the wedge in far enough to tighten the joint (be careful not to split the timber pole). Cut or plane off any excess wedge and tenon.

CHAMFERING THE BASE LEGS, POLE AND BRACES

12 Use a smoothing plane to plane a chamfer on the ends of each of the four base legs. Lay the pole on a suitable work surface. From the base,

11 Glue the wedge, insert it in the saw cut and use the hammer to drive the wedge in to tighten the joint.

measure up 250 mm and then measure up a further 1500 mm. With a combination square, square the marked lines around the pole. Using a pencil and your fingers as a gauge, mark lines 5 mm in, parallel to all the edges between the lines. At the end marks, use a chisel at 45 degrees to make small cuts in the edges of the pole. With the ground cutting edge down, working from about 25 mm in from each of the previous marks, make a chamfer back to the original mark. Use a smoothing plane or spokeshave to finish the chamfers between the marks. (Using a router with a chamfering bit is a faster method, or you could use an ovolo moulding bit for a fancy finish.)

13 For the braces, start the chamfer 50 mm in from each end on the outside edge only. Use the same process as for the pole, but reduce the chamfer width to 3 mm.

FINISHING

14 Sand the pole and braces with 180 grit abrasive paper. Paint the underside of the braces with the exterior clear finish. Start a 40 mm nail about 25 mm in from each end of the brace and apply a little adhesive to each joint face of the brace. Locate the brace centrally on the base leg and the pole, then finish nailing the brace to the base and pole. Repeat this step for all braces, and then place another nail in each joint. Measure 30 mm in from the end of each base leg and, in the centre at this point, drill an 8 mm hole through the timber. When positioning the post, a 6 mm steel tent peg about 300–450 mm long should be driven through this hole into the ground to stabilize the post.

15 Determine the height at which you will place the birdhouse or feeder, and cut the pole to the required length. Use the table on page 6 to establish the correct height.

16 Take the optional fixing plate and drill two 5 mm holes so it can be attached to the post, countersinking the holes to ensure the birdhouse will sit flat. Align the fixing plate and drill two 3 mm pilot holes for the screws. Attach the fixing plate with a little adhesive and two 50 mm countersunk screws. Drill a 5 mm hole near each corner, ready for fixing the birdhouse in position. Most birdhouses will require four 32 mm x 8 gauge brass woodscrews to secure them to the fixing plate.

17 Punch all the nail heads below the surface and use a suitable wood filler to fill any holes or gaps. Allow to dry before sanding with 180 grit abrasive paper.

18 Apply the first coat of exterior clear finish and leave to dry. Sand all the surfaces between each coat with 180 grit or finer abrasive paper – for the best results and the longest protection from the elements, use a minimum of three coats.

Clear acrylic sheets allow the seed supply to be monitored. Glass can be substituted, as long as any sharp edges have been smoothed off. Unlike acrylic material, glass will not craze with prolonged outdoor exposure.

Feeder with seed spreader

This is a practical and waste-free feeder, with an ingenious spreader design that allows only small quantities of seed to be dispensed. The lid can be removed for easy refilling and cleaning.

MATERIALS★

PART	MATERIAL	LENGTH	NO.
End	175 x 25 mm timber PAR	211 mm	2
Base	175 x 25 mm timber PAR	242 mm	1
Lid	100 x 25 mm timber PAR	300 mm	1
Roof panel	100 x 16 mm timber PAR	300 mm	2
Side	50 x 16 mm timber PAR	300 mm	2
Lid cleat	50 x 16 mm timber PAR	241 mm	1
Seed spreader	38 x 38 mm timber PAR	242 mm	1
Clear panel	145 x 6 mm acrylic sheet	260 mm	2

OTHER: Eight 25 mm nails; four 40 mm nails; ten 30 mm nails; four brass hooks; epoxy resin adhesive; water-based wood filler; abrasive paper: one sheet of 120 grit and one sheet of 180 grit; exterior clear acrylic paint; vegetable oil; required length of brass chain

Finished size: 300 mm long; 164 mm wide (without roof); 230 mm tall. Timber sizes given are nominal. For timber types and sizes see page 64.

CUTTING THE END AND BASE PIECES

1 Take the end piece timber and check that one edge is straight and square. From this edge use a marking gauge set to 140 mm to mark a line along the face. Clamp the timber to the work surface and cut along the waste side of the line with the panel saw. Place the end piece on edge in a vice and plane to the 140 mm line; ensure it is straight and square.

2 Square a line across the end piece, close to one end. Mark the length (211 mm). Leave a space of 5 mm and mark out 211 mm for the other end piece. Square the lines over the edge and across the back face.

3 Take the base piece timber and cut to 140 mm wide as in step 1. Mark off the length of 242 mm. With a utility knife, score the lines to cut the surface fibres, then cut to length.

TOOLS

- Combination square
- Measuring tape or fold-out rule
- Pencil
- Utility knife
- Marking gauge
- Quick-release cramp
- Crosscut or circular saw or jigsaw
- Tenon saw
- Vice
- Smoothing plane
- Hammer
- Set square: 30 degree
- Electric router
- Router bit: 6 mm straight
- Sliding bevel
- Electric drill (optional)
- Drill bit: 6 mm (optional)
- Cork sanding block or electric sander
- Nail punch

CUTTING THE ROOF PANELS AND SIDE PIECES

4 Take the roof panel timber and check the edge is straight and square. Use a marking gauge set to 91 mm to mark a line along the face. Clamp the piece down and use the crosscut saw to cut on the waste side of the line. Plane the rough edge straight and smooth. Dress the rough-sawn edges back to the correct width.

5 Square a line across one end of the roof panel timber and mark off two pieces at 300 mm, leaving a 5 mm space for saw cuts. Square the lines all around the timber. Score the lines with a utility knife and cut the pieces to length. Hold the two pieces of the same dimensions end upwards in a vice with length marks aligned. Plane the end grain back to the knife lines, planing from the outer edges towards the centre. Next, mark and cut to length the 41 mm wide side pieces.

MAKING GROOVED ENDS

6 Fasten the end pieces together with two 25 mm nails, end marks aligned. Place the pieces end upwards in a vice and plane them square across, then turn them other end upwards and repeat the process to bring the ends to the correct length.

7 Mark the centre of the top end of the pieces and square the line across both pieces. Measure out 17 mm from the centre line on each side. From there, use a 30 degree set square to mark the angled lines on

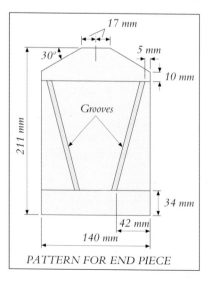

PATTERN FOR END PIECE

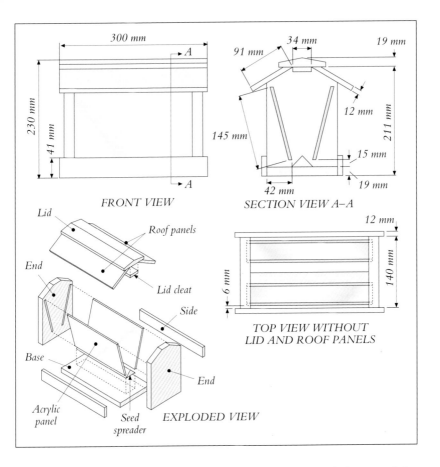

300 mm

A

230 mm

41 mm

A

FRONT VIEW

34 mm

91 mm

19 mm

12 mm

145 mm

211 mm

15 mm

42 mm

19 mm

SECTION VIEW A–A

Lid

Roof panels

End

Lid cleat

Side

6 mm

Base

End

Acrylic panel

Seed spreader

EXPLODED VIEW

12 mm

140 mm

TOP VIEW WITHOUT
LID AND ROOF PANELS

the end faces, on both sides. Square a line across the outer edges to ensure both sides are equal.

8 Score the lines with a utility knife and cut off the waste with a tenon saw. Place the ends in the vice and plane back to the angled lines. Tilt the ends so the angle line is quite level, and plane square to the face.

9 From the lower point of the angled end, measure down 10 mm

and in 5 mm to find the top of the groove. On the bottom of the end piece measure up 34 mm and in 42 mm: this is the bottom of the groove. Draw a line between the points to give the angle.

10 Find the distance from the edge of the router cutter to the edge of the router base (to find how far from the line you need to set the fence). Set to cut 10 mm deep. Nail a piece of straight timber parallel to the line

at the right distance. Practise plunge-routing on scrap timber first; check that the cutter will cut on the correct side of the line. Cut the grooves.

11 Set the sliding bevel to the angle formed between the lid position and the angled edge. Transfer this angle to the end of each roof panel. Start the end of the angle at the corner and draw the line to the opposite face. Set a marking gauge to this width and mark a line along the face of the board. Clamp the piece edge upwards in a vice and plane the angle. Repeat for the other panel.

MAKING THE SEED SPREADER

12 Place the seed spreader timber end upwards in a vice and use a crosscut saw to saw diagonally down the length to form a triangular section. Keep to one side of centre and cut straight. Turn the piece around to finish the cut. Plane the wide face smooth and straight. From a square end, mark and cut to a length of 242 mm. Mark a centre line from the apex of the triangle to the centre of the wide face at each end.

13 On the base, mark a centre line at each end. Apply adhesive to the bottom of the spreader, then align the centre line mark on both pieces. Hold the spreader in place with two 25 mm nails – remove when the adhesive has set.

14 Use a tenon saw or jigsaw with a fine-toothed blade to cut the acrylic sheet to size. Work slowly to minimize chipping (suppliers can cut acrylic panels to size for you). Keep the backing paper in place. Sand with 120 grit abrasive paper.

ASSEMBLING THE FEEDER

15 Sand all inside surfaces well with 120 grit abrasive paper. Hold the base piece end up, and align the end piece flush with the end and sides of the base. Fix with two 40 mm nails. Turn the base so the other end faces up. Remove the paper from the acrylic panels and insert them in the routed grooves. Glue and fix the other end with two 40 mm nails.

16 Position the feeder side upwards. Take the two side pieces and mark

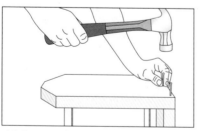

15 Insert the acrylic panels in the routed grooves. Glue and fix the other end with two 40 mm nails.

18 Nail cleats to the surface to steady the lid. Use a smoothing plane to bevel the top face.

10 mm in from each end. Glue and nail the first side piece to the feeder, flush with the base. There should be an overhang of 10 mm each end. Use three 30 mm nails to secure; repeat for the other side. The ends must remain square to the base.

17 Measure and mark 10 mm in from each end of the roof panels. Glue the angled cut on the end pieces. Align one roof panel, bevelled side upwards, flush with the flat section on the end piece and overhanging 10 mm each end. Fasten the panel with one 30 mm nail at each end. Repeat for the other panel.

18 The opening in the top of the feeder measures 242 x 34 mm. Using waste timber, cut a lid cleat slightly over-size and plane to fit. Take the 100 x 25 mm timber for the lid and mark a centre line down the length of the top face. Use a marking gauge to mark a line along each edge, 5 mm up from the bottom face. Draw a line on each end to represent the pitch on the lid. Place the lid in a vice, or nail cleats to the work surface to steady the lid. Use a smoothing plane to bevel the top face.

19 Mark a centre line on the underside of the lid, along its length. Next, mark a centre line on the ends of the lid cleat. Glue the adjoining face of the lid cleat and align the centre lines of the lid and cleat. Ensure there is an equal overhang, then fasten the cleat with two 25 mm

nails. Check the fit (use a smoothing plane to flush off the roof pieces so the lid sits hard down). Attach brass hooks 20 x 20 mm in from each corner of the roof.

FINISHING

20 Punch all nails below the surface, fill and leave to dry. Sand all exterior surfaces with 120 grit abrasive paper and finish with 180 grit.

21 Apply the first of three coats of paint to the outside surfaces. Sand back between coats with 180 grit abrasive paper. Apply two coats of vegetable oil to the inside surface.

EXTERIOR ADHESIVES

The best and most commonly available adhesive for outdoor projects is the epoxy resin type. It is a two-part adhesive: one part is the resin adhesive and the other part is the hardening agent required to set the resin. It comes in both a normal setting form (which takes about 24 hours to bond) and a quick-setting version (which sets in 5–10 minutes). The normal setting type is recommended, as the fast-curing adhesives often go hard before you can use the amount mixed. Polyvinyl acetate (PVA) or white woodworking glue should not be used as it will break down in the rain. Contact-type adhesives don't form a permanent bond outdoors.

These bevelled roof panels were carefully marked out using set squares and a sliding bevel. This birdhouse is made from waterproof A-grade plywood, and has been painted in contrasting colours that highlight its distinctive shape.

Birdhouse with bevelled roof panels

With its small entrance hole, this snug design offers smaller birds a haven from larger predators.

MATERIALS★

Part	Material	Finished length	Width	No.
Front/back	18 mm A-grade plywood	240 mm	220 mm	2
Side	18 mm A-grade plywood	164 mm	160 mm	2
Roof panel	18 mm A-grade plywood	240 mm	115 mm	4
Base	18 mm A-grade plywood	240 mm	220 mm	1

OTHER: Twenty 40 mm nails; four 35 mm x 8 gauge brass countersunk screws; one 50 x 8 mm timber dowel for the perch; small amount of epoxy resin adhesive; wood filler; one sheet of 180 grit abrasive paper; 500 ml exterior acrylic paint of your choice

★ Finished size: 240 mm long (base); 350 mm wide (roof); 280 mm high (from bottom of base to top of roof).

CUTTING OUT

1 With a combination square and measuring tape, mark out the parts, leaving 5 mm between each for saw cuts. Keep at least one edge of each part to the outer edge of the sheet.

2 With a circular saw or jigsaw, cut the parts – use a fence or rip guide to keep the saw travelling straight.

SETTING OUT THE FRONT AND BACK PIECES

3 Take the front and back pieces and temporarily nail them together with 40 mm nails, aligning bottom edges. Both should be just over 240 mm long by 220 mm wide. Mark the centre of the shorter bottom edge, then square a line up the centre of the length. Mark off 160 mm and 240 mm along this line. Square the lines from the 160 mm mark to the outer edges of the boards.

4 Place the attached front and back pieces together in a vice, then plane the sides straight and square to the bottom. Use a combination square, as well as the 30 degree angle and the

TOOLS

- Measuring tape or fold-out rule
- Combination square
- Pencil
- Portable circular saw or jigsaw
- Compass or protractor (optional)
- Set squares: 60/30 degrees, 45 degrees
- G-cramp or quick-release cramp
- Vice
- Hammer
- Smoothing plane
- Sliding bevel
- Marking gauge
- Electric drill
- Drill bits: 3 mm, 5 mm, 8 mm; 32 mm spade bit or hole saw
- Screwdriver (cross-head or recessed)
- Cork sanding block or electric sander
- Nail punch

45 degree angle on the set squares, to set out a 15 degree angle down from the 240 mm mark at the top centre position (or use a compass or protractor to set out the angles).

5 Using the 45 degree set square and the combination square, draw a line from the 160 mm marks on the outer edges to the 15 degree angle. This makes the intersecting angle. Repeat for the other side. Along the bottom edge, mark out 90 mm each side of the centre. Working from these marks, draw lines to join the 160 mm marks.

6 Keep the front and back pieces nailed together and clamp them to the workbench. Use a jigsaw to cut out the shape of the two pieces. Place them in the vice and plane them back to the lines with a smoothing plane, ensuring that the edges are square.

MAKING THE SIDE PIECES, ROOF PANELS AND BASE

7 Set the sliding bevel to the angle of the side, using the front/back pieces as a guide. Transfer this angle to the bottom edge of the side pieces at each end. With a marking gauge, mark the width of angle along the edge to be planed. Place the side piece in a vice and plane back to the gauged line. Repeat for the other side panel. Plane the side pieces back to their correct size, 164 x 160 mm, keeping the edges square.

8 Plane the roof panels to their correct size, 240 x 115 mm, keeping the edges square. Using the front/back pieces as a guide, set the sliding bevel to the mitre angle at the apex of the pieces. Transfer this angle

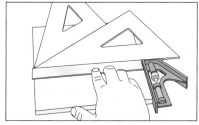

4 Use a combination square, and the 30 and 45 degree angle on the set squares, to set out a 15 degree angle.

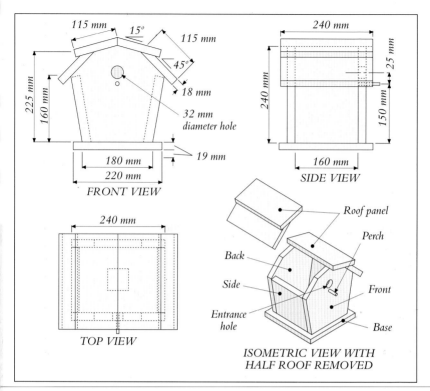

115 mm

15°

115 mm

45°

18 mm

32 mm
diameter hole

22.5 mm

160 mm

19 mm

180 mm

220 mm

FRONT VIEW

240 mm

25 mm

240 mm

150 mm

160 mm

SIDE VIEW

240 mm

TOP VIEW

Roof panel

Perch

Back

Side

Front

Entrance
hole

Base

ISOMETRIC VIEW WITH
HALF ROOF REMOVED

to the edges of two of the roof panels and mark the width of the angle along the edge to be planed. Place the panel in a vice and plane the angle. Repeat this process for the other panel.

9 Using the front/back pieces as a guide, set the sliding bevel to the intersecting angle. Transfer this angle to the edge of the two remaining roof panels. Use a marking gauge to mark the line along the length of the

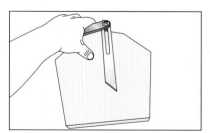

8 Using the front/back pieces as a guide, set the sliding bevel to the mitre angle at the apex of the pieces.

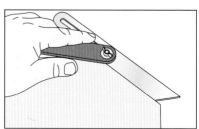

9 Set the sliding bevel to the intersecting angle. Transfer this angle to the edge of the roof panels.

panels, and then plane the angle on the pieces.

10 Plane the base back to its correct size of 220 x 240 mm, keeping the edges square.

ASSEMBLY

11 Mix up some adhesive following the manufacturer's instructions. Separate the nailed front and back pieces, and on the front piece where the sides are to be attached start two 40 mm nails 9 mm in from the edge. Take one side piece, glue the joining edge and then bring the front and side pieces together. Check to make sure that the bevelled edge of the side piece is flush with the bottom edge and side of the front piece. Finish by nailing the front piece to the side. Repeat this process for the remaining side and back pieces, to make a box shape. Ensure that the box is square.

12 Glue the lower angled edges at the top of the front and back pieces. Take the corresponding roof panels and start one 40 mm nail 29 mm in from each end of the panel. Align the roof panel on the box so the roof panel overhangs by 20 mm at each end. The bevelled edge must be flush with the top angle on the front and back pieces (see the diagram on page 61). Hammer in the nails. Repeat for the opposite roof panel. If the roof panels are not perfectly flush, wait until the adhesive sets and smooth them off with a smoothing plane.

13 Before fixing the remaining roof panels, check the fit. Ensure the mitre joint fits neatly. Glue the remaining joint edges and nail on the last two roof panels, keeping the ends flush and the mitres tight.

14 Lay the box face upwards. Measure 175 mm up the centre and mark the entrance hole position. Next, measure up 150 mm and mark the perch position. Use a 32 mm hole saw or a spade bit to make the entrance hole. For the perch, use an 8 mm drill bit to drill a hole 10 mm deep. Apply adhesive to the hole and insert the dowel.

15 Align the box on the base. Trace around the box to mark the outer edges on the base, then remove the box. Measure in 29 mm from the front and back edge of the base to centre the screw positions, then measure in 55 mm from each side edge. Where these points intersect, drill a 5 mm hole. On the underside of the base, countersink the holes. Rest the box on its roof and align the base on the box. Drill 3 mm pilot holes, then fasten the base to the box using four 35 mm screws. Drill four drainage holes in the base.

16 Punch all nails below the surface and apply wood filler to all holes and gaps, then sand the entire birdhouse with abrasive paper. Apply a coat of paint, then leave to dry before sanding and applying a second coat. A third coat of paint is advisable.

Tools for building birdhouses

Some of the most useful tools for making birdhouses are shown below. Build up your tool kit gradually – most of the tools can be purchased from your local hardware store.

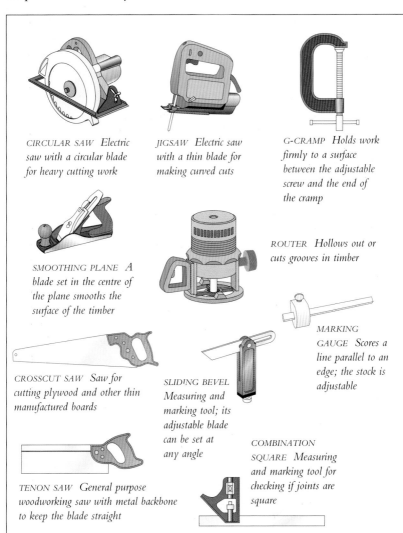

CIRCULAR SAW *Electric saw with a circular blade for heavy cutting work*

JIGSAW *Electric saw with a thin blade for making curved cuts*

G-CRAMP *Holds work firmly to a surface between the adjustable screw and the end of the cramp*

SMOOTHING PLANE *A blade set in the centre of the plane smooths the surface of the timber*

ROUTER *Hollows out or cuts grooves in timber*

CROSSCUT SAW *Saw for cutting plywood and other thin manufactured boards*

SLIDING BEVEL *Measuring and marking tool; its adjustable blade can be set at any angle*

MARKING GAUGE *Scores a line parallel to an edge; the stock is adjustable*

TENON SAW *General purpose woodworking saw with metal backbone to keep the blade straight*

COMBINATION SQUARE *Measuring and marking tool for checking if joints are square*

Index

A–B
adhesives, exterior, 57
bevelled roof panels,
  birdhouse with, 58
birdhouses
  designing, 7–8
  maintaining, 8–9
  siting, 7
  sizes of, 6–7
birds, attracting, 4–9

D
decorative birdhouses, 9
dovecote, 34

F–G
feeders, 5–7
  open-sided, 16
  with seed spreader, 52
  siting, 7
finishing products, 15
food for birds, 5–7
gabled birdhouse, 22

H
hanging birdhouse, 10
hinged lid, birdhouse
  with, 28
hollow log birdhouse, 42

O–P
open-sided feeder, 16
planing technique, 14
planning birdhouses and
  feeders, 4
post for birdhouses and
  feeders, 8, 46

R–S
routing technique, 45
seed spreader, feeder
  with, 52
supplementary feeding of
  birds, 5–7

TIMBER

Western red cedar and A-grade plywood were used extensively in this book. A-grade plywood is a waterproof product made up of laminations of timber veneers – 18 mm thickness has adequate insulating properties. For a good surface finish requiring little filling, use a B-grade veneer face. Western red cedar is the recommended timber for projects with a clear exterior finish – it outperforms other timbers used outdoors because of the resin, oils and tannins it contains. Never use treated pine for birdhouses or feeders, as it contains arsenic – many birds gnaw on timber, and the toxins in treated pine may eventually kill them. Chipboard and medium-density fibreboard will not withstand outdoor conditions.

TIMBER CONDITIONS
Timber is sold in three conditions:
- sawn or rough sawn: sawn to a specific (nominal) size
- planed, either planed all round (PAR), planed on two sides (P2S) or double planed
- moulded: planed to a specific profile for skirting boards and so on.
- Planed timber is mostly sold using the same nominal dimensions as sawn timber, for example 100 x 50 mm, but the surfaces have been machined to a flat, even width and thickness so the '100 x 50 mm' timber is really 91 x 41 mm. The chart shows actual sizes for seasoned timber; unseasoned timber such as pine will vary in size.

Sawn (nominal) size (mm)	Size after planing (mm)
16	12
19	15
25	19
38	30
50	41
75	66
100	91
125	115